Texts
Ingrid Sever

Contents

1 The detail is taken from the façade of one of the lovely houses in Zagreb built in Classical and Secessionist styles. The building is home to the Museum of Arts and Crafts.

2-3 Dubrovnik is a unique city. Its sixteenth-century walls are wonderfully well preserved and encircle the old city center that was the origin of the Republic of Ragusa.

4-5 Dancing girls wear the local costume decorated with fancy lacework and embroidery. Traditional customs are upheld in Croatia and there are many folkloric events across the country.

6 In Slavonia customs vary from zone to zone. The girl in the photograph is showing off one with evident satisfaction and a great deal of grace.

7 The monument to August Senoa, one of Croatia's most famous nineteenth-century writers, in Zagreb. Of his many works, the historical novels were the most widely read.

8-9 Povlje is a village in the northeast of the island of Brac. Nearby there are the ruins of a basilica and a baptistery from the fifth and sixth centuries. Behind we see the jagged and mountainous coastline.

© 2004 White Star S.r.l.
Via C. Sassone, 22/24
13100 Vercelli, Italy
www.whitestar.it

ISBN 88-544-0027-0

REPRINTS:
2 3 4 5 6   08 07 06 05 04

TRANSLATION
Timothy Stroud

Printed in Singapore by Star Standard
Color separation: Chiaroscuro, Turin

Introduction

Croatia is a land of red roofs in fields and meadows, alpine landscapes that run down to the sea and, most of all, of islands: the people who live there reflect the colors and peculiarities of the nature that surrounds them. The natural environment reigns unchallenged in Croatia where contrasting landscapes of gentle and violent characters meet and blend, but it is the sea along the long coastline that dominates the nature of the land.

Politically, Republic of Croatia was established in 1991 following the dissolution of Yugoslavia. It has a tormented history that originated with the wave of Slavs that arrived around the seventh century. Then, beginning in the ninth century, it was the turn of the Croat princes and kings whose traces are left in the epigraphs they had carved using glagolitic script.

Remains of the Roman civilization and the influence of other peoples that have played a significant role in the history of the region can still be seen along the coast and occasionally inland.

Like all wars, the 'War of Independence' of 1991 damaged the country's society and artistic heritage. Reconstruction and restoration of buildings began soon after peace was achieved but are still in progress. However, it is much more difficult to heal the scars suffered by the people during the war. The wounds left by the violence are still perceptible in the looks and faces of the citizens, especially on those who lived where the war was cruelest.

Geographically and climatically Croatia is divided into continental Croatia, alpine Croatia and Mediterranean Croatia. The continental region covers the Pannonic plain in the north and northeast of the country and the zone of the Slavonian plain between the Drava and Sava rivers. In the northwest is the hilly Zagorje area.

The continental climate is transmuted into its alpine equivalent in the south and southwest, in the areas of Bania, Kordun, Lika, the Dinar Mountains and the wooded Gorski Kotar. Mediterranean Croatia runs along the marvelous 1,100 miles of coastline made up of bays, inlets and more than a thousand islands.

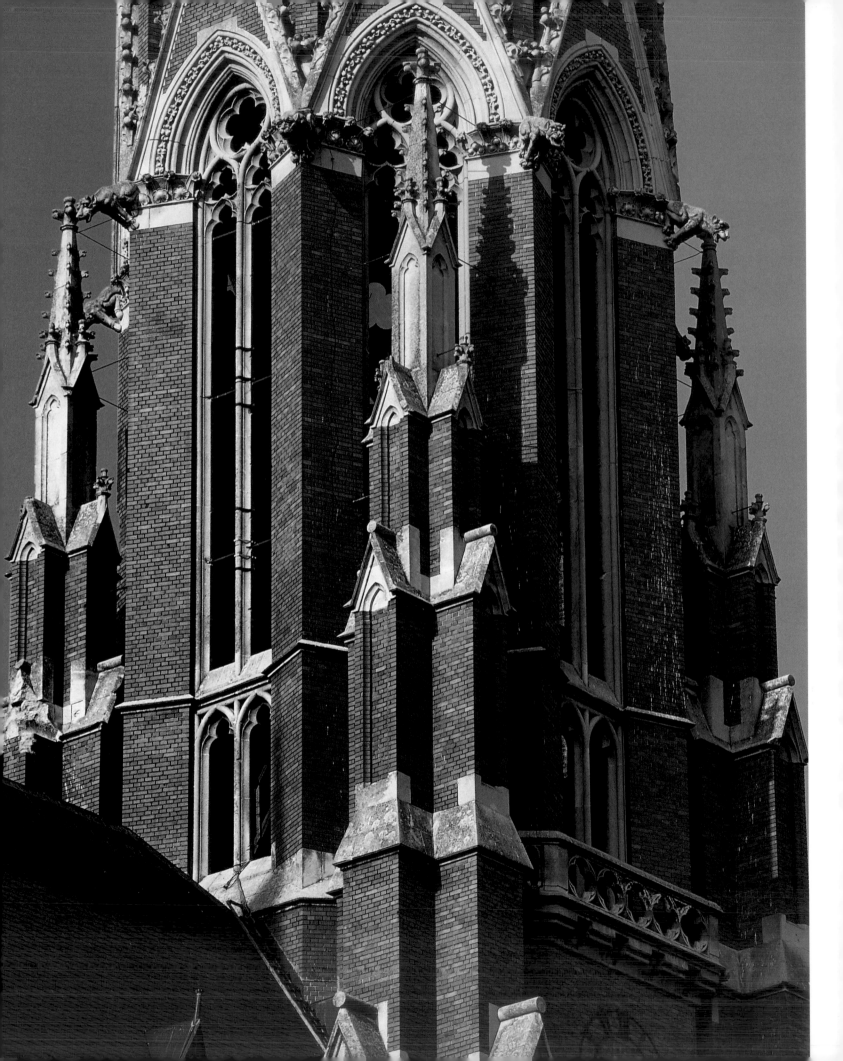

10 Built at the end of the ninth century in Neo-Gothic style, the cathedral of Saints Peter and Paul in Osijek was built at the instigation of bishop J.J. Strossmayer.

11 top The medieval castle in Varazdin (Stari Grad) was rebuilt in the sixteenth century in Renaissance style.

11 bottom The Kaptol in Zagreb is one of the two villages around which the capital of Croatia was developed. The Kaptol has always been a bishopric: the statue in the square is dedicated to the Madonna.

The political and administrative capital of Croatia is Zagreb, which is home to almost one million inhabitants. Zagreb formally came into being in 1094 when King Ladislav founded the bishopric, but we know that its origins are older than this because remains of an Illyrian settlement and Roman military camp have been discovered. The city was located on the road that leads from the Baltic Sea to the Adriatic Sea. In 1557 Zagreb was 'the most important city' in the kingdom of Croatia and Slavonia. Its major economic growth resulted from the rise in industry and commerce during the second half of the nineteenth century. This was when its most beautiful buildings in Baroque, Neo-Classical and Secessionist styles were constructed.

Today the city is fast moving. The old city center, where there are dozens of cafés, beer-houses and meeting places, has always been packed with people. Its streets, squares, markets and fairs are typical of a bustling commercial city but there is also a cultural side with busy museums, art galleries and theaters. Examples of lovely eighteenth-century buildings in Zagreb are the Banski Dvori, which have been turned into the building of the Governement (Council of the Ministers).

The predominant faith in Croatia is Catholic, and the point of reference for all Catholic Croats is the Kaptol in Zagreb where the cathedral stands.

Outside the city in the area known as Zagorje, the landscape is very picturesque. Gentle vine-lined hills are dotted with red-roofed houses and small Baroque churches, then, down on the plain, there is the city of Varazdin, a pearl of Croatian Baroque with churches and late-eighteenth-century townhouses. The area has many castles (Veliki Tabor, Trakoscan, Bosiljevo, Brezovica, Klenovnik and Stari grad-Varazdin) that were built first as fortresses and then were partly rebuilt in the eighteenth century to become residences of the nobility.

Further north, on the border with Hungary, the city of Cakovec lies between the Mura and Drava rivers in the zone where the customs of the Croats blend with those of the Hungarians. To the east, towards Slavonia, the plain is covered with willow trees and the small fields are interspersed with the meadows and hunting grounds of Moslavina and there are also several spas in the area such as Daruvar and Lipik.

Set in the wheat fields of the plain there are towns like Dakovo, with its bishop's palace and cathedral with two bell-towers, and Osijek, a sixteenth-century town that was heavily influenced by the Turks but that today reflects Baroque and Secessionist styles. Further on are the cities of Vinkovci and Vukovar, the latter sadly famous for the tragic events of the war is also the location of the nearby archeological site of Vucevdol that dates to 2000 BC.

The area slowly flattens out towards the large rivers of the Danube (which marks the eastern border of Croatia) and the Drava, which flows through the reed bed of Kopacki rit. This is a nesting site for marsh birds and an observation area for ornithologists.

Returning along the Sava River, the area is very marshy. Between Sisak and Nova Gradiska, in the nature park of Lonjsko Polje, there lies one of the largest and best conserved wetlands in Europe. The roofs of the local wooden houses in the zone that stretches as far as Pozega are favorite nesting places for storks that return there year after year. All around there are large oak woods.

Another nature reserve worth mentioning is Medvenica Park that encompasses a mountain just north of Zagreb that features caves, waterfalls, canyons and woods of beech and fir trees. To the south, before heading into the mountains, is the city of Karlovac, which is known as "the city of four rivers" as it is situated where the Kupa, Korana, Dobra and Mreznica meet. Further south from here is where alpine Croatia begins.

The vast highland plateau of Gorski Kotar – in particular the national park of the Risnjak massif – is one of the loveliest unspoilt zones in Croatia. This provides a habitat for brown bears, lynxes, chamois, deer and eagles. The landscape is an expanse of fir woods whose dark green contrasts with the cheerful pale green of the meadows and grasslands.

The area is not very populated as the villages are set out along the road from Rijeka to Zagreb or from Zagreb to Dalmatia. This is the area of villages like Delnice, Cabar, Skrad, Vrbovsko, Lokve and Fuzine, with their splendid lakes, or Ogulin, Otocac and Gospic and the town of Lika. Each center has its own traditions and local dishes based on the natural resources of the area.

Gorski Kotar and Lika are silent zones where the only sounds are provided by the many species of birds. Lika is the region of Croatia's most beautiful national park, Plitvice Lakes, which has been designated a World Heritage site by UNESCO. It is formed by sixteen small lakes connected by waterfalls and streams that run through woods of fir and birch. Here you are in close contact with nature.

The land of the coastline falls sheer away into the sea. Close by stands the Velebit massif, with the Velika and Mala Paklenica ravines, karstic terrain and caves. The Velebit massif is home to a wide variety of protected plants and animals, some of which are endemic. A sort of botanic garden has been created here that nature-lovers and hikers enjoy visiting.

Krka National Park runs alongside the Krka River that flows through gorges and waterfalls, for example, Skradin and Roski and past the island of

Visovac where there is a fifteenth-century Franciscan monastery.

In the hinterland of Dalmatia stands the city of Knin, where there is a medieval fort linked to the kings of Croatia, and the city of Sinj, which every year commemorates the siege by the Turks with a knightly tournament called the Alka.

Further south, close by the sea and above the Makarska Riviera, stands the majestic white Mount Biokovo. It is home to innumerable varieties of plants and animals, in particular, the chamois. It is considered a nature park.

12-13 *Krka National Park covers the entire length of the river.*

13 bottom left *On the highland of Gorski Kotar, about 9 miles from the sea, the wooded Mount Risnjak represents the point where the continental and Mediterranean climates meet.*

13 bottom right *The rocky massif of Mount Biokovo was made a nature park to protect its flora and fauna.*

14-15 *The sixth-century mosaics of the Euphrasian basilica of Porec is clearly influenced by Byzantine architecture and resembles the historic buildings of Ravenna.*

At this point our journey takes us to the sea. Much of Croatia is bounded by the Mediterranean. Despite the cold winds from the northeast, the winters are mitigated by the sea while the heat of the southern sun in summer is cooled by the evening breeze. The clean, clear seawater reflects the rocks of the coast and caresses the pebbles of the endless beaches.

The journey starts from Istria, a peninsula in the shape of a triangle. Passing along the coast from the Gulf of Savudrija, we cross the towns of Umag and Novigrad, which, like all Istrian coastal towns, have experienced strong growth in tourism in recent years. Over the centuries the peninsula has been dominated by various powers and boasts traces of the Romans, Byzantines and Venetians. Porec is the site of an early Christian monument, the Euphrasian Basilica, which has superbly conserved mosaics, and the town's historic houses strongly resemble the palaces of Venice.

Istria has many churches of beauty, for example, the small church of Beram, famous for its medieval frescoes, the famous church of St. Euphemia in Rovigno and the duomo of St. Biagio (St. Blaise) in Vodnjan, with its collection of sacred art.

Pula is the largest city in Istria and had a glorious history under the Romans. Its arena (first-century AD amphitheater) is still visited and there are the Arch of the Sergi and Temple of Augustus in the ancient Roman forum.

Inland, Pazin is the administrative center of Istria, with Montecuccoli castle and its famous funnel-shaped karstic well. All of Istria is studded with hill-top villages that have almost been abandoned, for example, Hum, Plomin, Motovun, Groz?njan and others. The hills themselves have been cultivated with vines since the time of the Romans.

The east coast of Istria is dominated by Mount Ucka covered by pines and fir woods.

At its feet stand villages like Moscenica, Lovran and Opatija, which have been holiday resorts since the mid-nineteenth century. Opatija has hotels built in fin-de-siècle style that were an attraction to the nobility of Europe during the winter season. The coast is lined with laurel and myrtle and the paths alongside the sea make unforgettable walks.

A few miles separate Rijeka's abbey from the busy city itself, which is a center of communications for the area. The ancient port has a civic tower, a Roman arch, the cathedral of St. Vitus and the church of the Assumption of Our Lady. On the hill of Trsat on the far side of the Rijecina River is a long flight of steps that leads to the Sanctuary of the Madonna and the castle that belonged to the Frankopan counts.

16-17 The monumental Renaissance chapel dedicated to the Blessed Giovanni Orsini is found in the cathedral of Trogir. He is represented on a fourteenth-century sarcophagus (center).

17 top The exterior of the apse in the cathedral of St. James is decorated with the heads of 74 citizens of Sibenik.

17 bottom The Venetian lion of St. Mark in Zadar dominates the Terraferma Gate: this is a Renaissance work by Michele Sammicheli from 1543.

The coast road continues through bays, inlets, beaches and little ports like Bakar, Kraljevica and Crikvenica. The zone is bathed with lush Mediterranean vegetation, laurels, ilex and aromatic grasses. After the greenery of the Crikvenica Riviera, Novi Vinodolski and Senj, the landscape becomes harsh and rough. The sun burns the rocks and the land is swept by the Sirocco and Bora winds all the way down to Karlobag.

The jagged coast often hides its beauty from the inattentive visitor, but the hidden corners are jewels that deserve to remain hidden, to impress the observer all the more when they are finally discovered: delightful bays, sun-dappled inlets and rocks warmed by the sun.

After ancient Nin – the seat of the ancient bishops of Croatia – comes Zadar. One of the town's loveliest monuments is the pre-Romanesque church dedicated to St. Donatus. Romanesque architecture is represented by St. Mary's basilica, which has a collection of sacred art, and the cathedral of St. Anastasia from the twelfth and thirteenth centuries. Also worthy of a visit are the church of St. Simeon, the Renaissance Terraferma Gate and the city's museums. Although Zadar was heavily bombed during World War II, its streets and houses reveal its Venetian period. The next city on the route, after Biograd na moru, is Sibenik, dominated by the old fort of St. Anne. There are several palaces (Palazzo Foscolo and Palazzo Orsini) and many churches to visit, including the cathedral of St. James with its façade carved with the faces of citizens who lived there in the Middle Ages.

In Dalmatia the sea has served as a bridge between peoples of different cultures. The region itself first belonged to the Illyrians, then the Romans, the Byzantines, the Turks, the Croats and the Austro-Hungarian Empire. During its period of Venetian dominance, the continual maritime contacts it had with the Serenissima are reflected in its architecture and artistic heritage.

Continuing the trip, we pass through the ecclesiastical Trogir, founded by Syracusan colonists. The duomo of St. Laurence has an elegant bell-tower and is one of the most beautiful works of Romanesque style in Dalmatia; it contains paintings by Italian artists of the Baroque era (di Palma the Younger, Padovanino and others). Also deserving of a visit is the fourteenth-century loggia in Piazza dei Signori.

Across the Riviera of the Seven Castles you come to Split. This city was founded around Diocletian's palace of which four gateways can still be seen; the most beautiful is the Golden Gate in the north that led to the Roman town of Salona. The area around the palace has provided many archeological finds that today can be seen in the city's museums. Split is Dalmatia's most important city and main port and lies at the foot of the pine-clad Mount Marian. Its palm-fringed esplanade makes a lovely promenade.

The attractive riviera of Makarska on the slopes of Mount Biokovo is also lined with palms. It stands on the road to Dubrovnik and has become a well-known tourist resort. Passing over the mouth of the Neretva River and a zone of citrus groves and orchards, we cross the peninsula of Peljesac with its vineyards and wines.

Dubrovnik lies at the southern tip of Croatia. The city is divided in two by the Stradun – the main street that runs from Pila Gate to the Clock Tower and Mint in Piazza Loggia. This is the location of the duomo and Rectors' palace. The churches of St. Dominic and St. Francis (the latter with an ancient pharmacy inside) have superb cloisters built in Italian Renaissance style. In almost all the churches of the city you will see paintings by famous artists. The city was a maritime republic and in consequence was surrounded by fortifications with gates and towers. Visitors can still walk on its walls. Today Dubrovnik is a popular international tourist resort. Just in front of the city lies the lovely tiny island of Lokrum that used to belong to Maximilian and Rudolf Hapsburg.

There are many islands in Croatia and almost all of them are typical of the Mediterranean. They have dry walls, olive and almond groves, vineyards and fig and peach orchards. Where there is no cultivation, the Mediterranean vegetation prospers and myrtle and juniper bushes alternate with ilexes, pines and cypresses. Flocks of sheep are very common and the zone is famous for its cheeses.

A national park lies on the western side of the island of Mljet and incorporates two strips of sea called lakes. Here, on a small island, is a twelfth-century Benedictine abbey.

On the island of Korcula it is obligatory to visit St. Mark's cathedral and see the ancient knights' dance known as Moresca, which derives from a tradition practiced by the inhabitants relating to battles against the Turks. At Badija is a monastery with a beautiful cloister.

The town of Hvar on the island of the same name was an important Venetian port on the route to the east, which is why its houses have elegant Venetian façades. Hvar is also known for its ancient theater in

the main square, and beyond the cathedral you can see the seventeenth-century shipyard. In summer the island is filled with the color and perfume of lavender.

The Modra spilja on the island of Vis is a famous blue grotto. The beach at Bol, on the island of Brac, is an expanse of white pebbles lining a transparent sea. Further north is a series of islands in the Kornati archipelago, including Telascica nature park on Dugi otok (Long Island), which is a paradise for nature lovers. This is a great place for diving and admiring the sea bed.

Continuing north, we come to the island of Pag, known for its salt mines, bobbin lace and excellent sheep cheese.

The island of Rab boasts a number of tourist resorts but the curiosity of the visitor will be drawn by its Venetian-style town center, in particular the loggia, portals, Romanesque churches and four bell-towers.

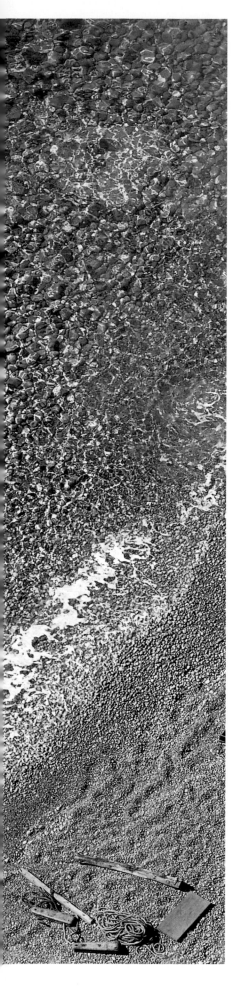

22-23 The noise of the surf and waves on the pebbles, the clear blue water and the toil of the fishermen are the sights and sounds along all of the Dalmatian coast.

23 top A fisherman deals with his net. Fishing has always been a source of income and nourishment for the people who live by the sea.

23 bottom Vrana Lake lies in the windswept zone at the center of the island of Cres. Its bottom lies 220 feet beneath sea level and its freshwater provides drinking water for most of the island's inhabitants.

The largest of the Quarnero Islands is Krk, with its delightful villages of Vrbnik and Dobrinj. The island also has Roman remains but is especially famous for the earliest example of Croatian script, which dates to the eleventh century and can be seen on the stone of Baska. The stone has inscriptions in glagolitic, which is an ancient Croatian alphabet. Near Punat, the tiny island of Kosljun has a monastery, and close to the capital of Krk stands the ancient church of St. Donato.

Tourist facilities are present in Njivice, Malinska and Baska, where a long beach lies at the foot of the mountains.

The island of Cres is like a natural oasis and is the habitat of the griffin, a protected species. In the middle of the island is a freshwater lake that provides water for the entire island. In winter the island is sparcely populated but in summer its villages of Valun, Lubenice and Martinscica return to life. Valun has a collection of epigraphs with all the most important examples of glagolitic script found on the islands and east coast of Istria.

At Osor a bridge connects Cres to the island of Losinj. This island features lush vegetation, the smells of the pine resin and balsamic grasses and, in summer, the whirring of the cicadas. Its towns of Mali Losinj and Veli Losinj have a long and glorious history of navigation and shipbuilding.

The island of Susak, the 'island of sand', produces a very particular wine and has a traditional brightly colored traditional dress worn by the girls.

The trip around Croatia is winding to an end. It started on the tiny island of Lokrum and will conclude on the islands of the Brijuni archipelago, which is a national park. The larger of the two islands was a luxury tourist resort at the start of the twentieth century, with its large houses and Roman, Byzantine and Venetian remains. The park is home to animals from all over the world that were given as gifts to President Tito, who often resided on the island.

And here the journey finishes. However, visitors will take away memories of the ruddy faces of the inhabitants of Slavonia and Zagorje and the costumes and dances of the local bands. They will have been impressed by the simple but human cordiality of the mountain people and the closeness of their life to nature. But most of all they will remember the artistic and natural beauty along the coast, the blue of the sea and the sun-wrinkled faces of the coastal people, their direct manner and their eyes that see into the distance.

Hungary

DRAVA

SLATINA

SLAVONIA

NASICE

OSIJEK

POZEGA

DAKOVO

DANUBE

Serbia

VUKOVAR

NOVA GRADISKA

VINKOVCI

SLAVONSKI
BROD

SAVA

ZUPANJA

SAVA

Bosnia
Herzegovina

Montenegro

PLOCE

PELJESAC

SLANO

MLJET

DUBROVNIK

A

25 top left The Clock Tower, also known as the Civic Tower, is the symbol of the modern city of Rijeka. It was built in 1750 on the site of an ancient gate.

25 top right A woman in traditional Slavonian costume. Considered the 'granary' of Croatia, Slavonia is the easternmost region of the country.

26-27 The sixteen lakes of Plitvice flow into one another creating lovely waterfalls. The entire surrounding area along the main road between Zagreb and Dalmatia is under the protection of UNESCO.

28-29 Kornati (crowned) archipelago is composed of many islands and strangely shaped and colored cliffs (there are 125). The crystal clear sea is an invitation to divers.

25

Continental Croatia

30 top Varazdin is one of the cities that have maintained their Baroque buildings unspoiled.

30 bottom The countryside of Croatian Zagorje is lined with vineyards that produce locally famous wines.

31 The photograph shows the top of one of the two bell-towers in Zagreb cathedral. They stand 338 and 344 feet tall.

Continental landscapes

32 *Trakoscan is a romantic castle that overlooks a lake and is surrounded by a park.*

33 top left *The castle has been renovated several times over the centuries. It was rebuilt completely in Neo-Gothic style by count Djuro Draskovic between 1853–56.*

34-35 *Veliki Tabor is one of the best conserved medieval forts in Croatia. Its Gothic–Renaissance nucleus is a pentagon enclosed by fortified walls. The monumental castle is perched on a hill overlooking pretty countryside.*

33 top right *Inside the castle of Trakoscan there is a library, an archive and various paintings and portraits of noblemen.*

33 bottom left *An attractive corner of the castle that had its origins in the fourteenth century.*

33 bottom right *Today the castle is a museum of furniture and objects from Croatia's feudal period.*

36 The highland plateau of Gorski Kotar and Risnjak park are an area of great natural beauty. It is inhabited by various species of animal that live undisturbed by man in the vast expanses of woods and grassland.

37 top The small village of Fu_ine with its artificial lake has recently become one of the principal tourist attractions of Gorski Kotar.

37 center Vrbovsko has a path 2 miles long that dawdles alongside a pretty stream.

37 bottom The lush vegetation is reflected in the waters. In this area it is possible to hunt, fish or go skiing in winter.

38 top In spring Slavonia is covered with expanses of green cornfields.

38 bottom The corn turns yellow and is ready for harvesting. Slavonia is Croatia's largest wheat provider.

38-39 Slavonia is a fertile, flattish region bounded by the rivers Sava, Drava and Danube. Agriculture here produces mostly cereals, fodder and fruit.

40-41 Grapes and fruit are grown on the hills of Zagorje, while the mountains nearby are lined with woods.

41 top Each village in Zagorje is characterized by a church and belltower. The best-known religious building in the area is to be seen in Marija Bistrica.

41 bottom The gentle green countryside of Zagorje is colored by the houses that dot the landscape.

Zagreb

42 The city of Zagreb, capital of Croatia, experienced rapid growth commercially, culturally, industrially and administratively in the eighteenth century.

43 top left The center of Zagreb – one of the loveliest capitals in eastern Europe – has many monumental buildings.

43 bottom left This is the 'Lower City' in Zagreb.

43 top right Mimara Museum has a varied collection of more than a thousand items from every era and area.

43 center right The church of St. Catherine was built by the Jesuits between 1620 and 1631. It is one of the most beautiful examples of Baroque architecture in Croatia.

43 bottom right The Museum of Arts and Crafts in Zagreb. The Lower City has many cultural institutes and museums.

44 top Zagreb's main square, Ban Jelacic, is lined with lovely townhouses and palaces.

44 center left Neo-Classical decorations adorn the entrance to a building in Strossmayer Avenue.

44 center right Street artists are often to be seen in Zagreb's squares; this is one in Ban Jelacic Square.

44 bottom Ban Jelacic Square is a busy center in Zagreb and a popular meeting place.

44-45 Ban Jelacic was a figure of notable importance in the history of the Croatian nation. His equestrian monument stands in the center of the square.

The Cathedral

46-47 *The cathedral of Zagreb is one of Croatia's most important religious buildings. It was renovated several times between the thirteenth and seventeenth centuries, resulting in the replacement of the Renaissance bell-tower by the two towers seen today. The portal was demolished and several Baroque altars were transferred to other churches. This is its magnificent interior.*

47 top *The Crucifixion at Golgotha is a sculpture just inside the cathedral.*

47 center left *The Madonna in a painting of 1610.*

47 center right *The tomb of the Blessed Alojzije Stepinac is visited by many Croat believers.*

47 bottom *The cathedral's treasure includes many precious objects donated by the bishops of Zagreb.*

48 left Jesuits' Square (Jezuitski trg) is part of a set of buildings built by the Jesuits that comprised their monastery, academy and refectory.

48 right One of the many monuments in Zagreb shows St. George killing the dragon.

49 left Walking through Zagreb, one often halts to admire a detail on the many palaces.

49 top right The old Tkalcic Street (seen in the photograph) joined the hamlet of Gradec to the hamlet of Kaptol.

49 bottom right The stone gate (Kamenita vrata) marked the entrance to Gradec. A votive image of the Madonna is seen inside the gate.

The Kaptol

50 The photograph shows one of the four gilded angels on the fountain of the Blessed Virgin in the Kaptol.

51 top The statue dedicated to the Blessed Virgin stands on a column and overlooks the cathedral square.

51 bottom The Kaptol has always represented the power of the Church in Zagreb. In the past it was surrounded by walls but these have now been mostly substituted with palaces.

Hrvatsko Narodno Kazaliste (Croatian National Theater)

52 top left The National Theater was designed in 1893 by the Viennese architects Helmer and Fellner.

52 top right In the space in front of the theater there is a Secessionist composition by Ivan Mestrovic called The Well of Life (Zdenac zivota).

52 bottom The photograph shows the beauty of the sculpture on the top of the theater's main façade.

53 Splendid reliefs decorated the façade of the Croatian National Theater where the first Croation operas were performed in the second half of the nineteenth century.

St. Mark's Church

54 top left The interior of the church of St. Mark is decorated with cycles of frescoes.

54 top right The image of the Madonna is widely worshiped in Croatia. A window in St. Mark's church shows her with the Child and saints.

54 center left The Gothic church of St. Mark, with its Baroque bell-tower, stands in the center of the 'upper city' in Zagreb.

54 center right St. Mark's is one of Zagreb' most important parish churches. This is part of the façade.

54 bottom The coat of arms of Zagreb is displayed on the roof of St. Mark's.

54-55 The roof tiles installed in 1880 reproduce the medieval coat of arms of Croatia, Dalmatia and Slavonia.

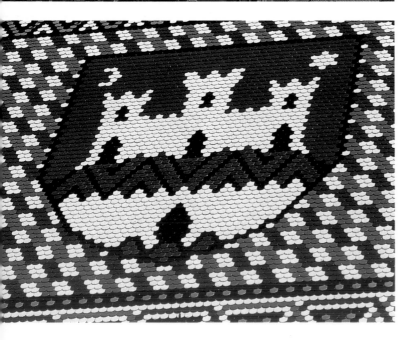

Varazdin

56-57 *Varazdin originated as a fort (today called Stari Grad) and the town grew up around it. Until the devastating fire of 1776, it was the principal city of the banate of Croatia.*

57 top left *Varazdin is the Croatian capital of Baroque architecture; the style is clearly seen in the details on the exteriors of its minor churches.*

57 top right *The church of St. Nicholas has a Gothic bell-tower dated 1491 on which the city's coat of arms is carved.*

57 center *The more important churches in Varazdin are those of the Assumption, the Capuchin church of the Holy Trinity, and the Franciscan church of St. John the Baptist.*

57 bottom *The square kralj Tomislav in Varazdin is surrounded by Baroque buildings that provide the city with its very special atmosphere.*

58

58-59 *The Madonna is painted on the sundial on a wall of the church of St. John the Baptist.*

59 top left *The statue is of Gregory of Nin, a charismatic Croat bishop who lived in the tenth century.*

59 top right *The church of St. John the Baptist stands close to the Franciscan monastery that contains various paintings, a library and a pharmacy.*

59 center left *This caryatid decorates the façade of the theater in Varazdin.*

59 center right *Varazdin has ancient musical traditions. Each year it gives many concerts, including the 'Baroque evenings' festival. This is the Croat National Theater in Varazdin.*

59 bottom *The cemetery in Varazdin is a well-cared-for garden in which hedges are grown as partitions.*

Osijek

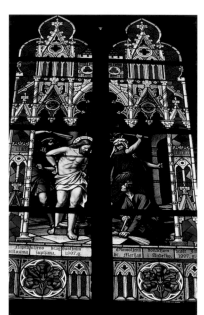

60 top The church of Saints Peter and Paul has a magnificent organ.

60 center left The brick church of Saints Peter and Paul was built at the instigation of bishop Strossmayer.

60 center right One of the windows in the church shows the Way of the Cross.

60 bottom A detail on the façade of the cathedral shows a griffin.

60-61 The frescoes inside were painted by Mirko Racki.

Other cities

62-63 *Cakovec is the main city in Medimurje. The medieval city was heavily influenced by its aristocratic Hungarian owners, Zrinski, Althani and Festetics.*

63 top left *One of the bell-towers on the bastion in Cakovec was built in the eighteenth century.*

63 top right *The church of the Holy Trinity stands next to the barracks in the main square in Karlovac, with the seventeenth-century Franciscan monastery next to it.*

63 center *The 'Stari dvor of the Zrinski's is a series of palaces that have been turned into a museum.*

63 bottom *Karlovac was built as a fortified city on marshy ground. These gardens substituted the city bastions.*

64-65 *This is the splendid interior of the cathedral of St. Peter built at the instigation of the bishop of Djakovo, Josip Juraj Strossmajer, whose remains lie in the crypt.*

65 *The Neo-Romanesque cathedral of St. Peter in Djakovo was designed by K. Roesner and F. Schmidt in the second half of the nineteenth century. Its bell-towers are 275 feet tall.*

The Coast and Dalmatia

66 top *The shoreline of Split is lined with palms. The cathedral bell-tower can be seen in the distance.*

66 bottom *The Roman city of Ad Turres became today's Crikvenica, a tourist resort with a pleasant riviera.*

67 *The high defensive walls of Dubrovnik were built right over the sea.*

Crikvenica Riviera

68-69 *Rocky inlets and bays with pebble beaches: the landscape is a little harsh but the sea is clean and blue.*

69 top *Crikvenica Riviera has a very mild climate, and it was here that the first Croatian bathing resorts sprang up.*

69 center *A seaside beach with sunshades. Crikvenica is a growing tourist resort.*

69 bottom *A stretch of the coast between Crikvenica and Rijeka. The area is well-equipped with tourist facilities.*

Nin and Zadar

70-71 *The church of St. Donatus belongs to a pre-Romanesque period and is 85 feet tall. It is thought to have been built in the first half of the ninth century by bishop Donatus.*

71 top *This is the pre-Romanesque architecture on an irregular plan of one of the oldest churches in Nin: the Holy Cross, dating to the tenth century.*

71 center left *A tower was built on the dome of the church of St. Nicholas in Nin to act as a lookout point during the war against the Turks.*

71 center right *The cathedral of St. Anastasia in Zadar is an eleventh-century basilica. It conserves the sarcophagus of the saint in the left apse.*

71 bottom *The 'Sea Gate' in Zadar features a large lion of St. Mark's. It dates to 1573 and was built to commemorate the victory at Lepanto by the Venetian fleet over the Turks.*

Sibenik

72 The Renaissance roof of the cathedral of Sibenik was built in stone from the islands of Dalmatia. The picture shows the statue of St. Michael, the patron saint of the city.

73 left St. James' cathedral in Sibenik is one of the largest religious buildings on the east coast of the Adriatic.

73 top right Sibenik cathedral has several altars with sculptures and reliefs by Niccolò Fiorentino and Juraj Petrovic, and paintings by Bernardino Ricci.

73 bottom right The historic center is a maze of alleys and stairways that climb the hill. The 'Lords' Square' is lined with Venetian style palaces.

Trogir

74 The Trg Ivana Pavla II is the central square in Trogir, onto which some of the city's loveliest buildings face, including the superb fourteenth-century Public Loggia.

75 top This is one of the 160 statues on the vault or in the niches of the chapel dedicated to the Blessed St. John of Trogir in the cathedral of Sv. Lovro (St. Laurence).

75 bottom St. Laurence's cathedral is a basilica with a nave, two aisles and three apses. Its bell-tower combines Romanesque, Gothic and Renaissance architecture.

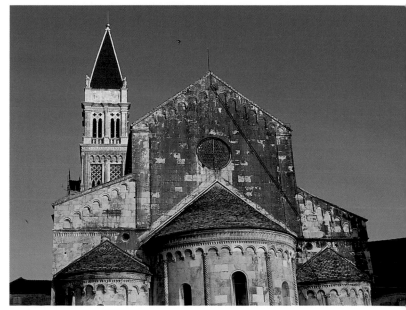

Split

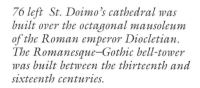

76 left St. Doimo's cathedral was built over the octagonal mausoleum of the Roman emperor Diocletian. The Romanesque–Gothic bell-tower was built between the thirteenth and sixteenth centuries.

76 top right A detail of the foot of Gregory of Nin (Grgur Ninski). The statue was executed by Ivan Mestrovic.

76 bottom right A thirteenth-century pulpit by an unknown artist stands to the left of the entrance to the cathedral.

77 The Silver Gate in Diocletian's Palace is the city's east gate. The largest gate is the northern one, known as the Golden Gate.

78 Night-time in Split: the bell-tower of St. Doimo's (Sveti Duje) is lit up at the center of the photograph.

78-79 The opera Aida is performed in the peristyle of Diocletian's Palace. Split puts on many cultural events in the summer.

Makarska Riviera

80 top The road follows the coast and offers typically Mediterranean views.

80 bottom Makarska riviera has many inlets and rocky ravines.

80-81 Makarska port in early evening: the fishing boats prepare to go out to sea.

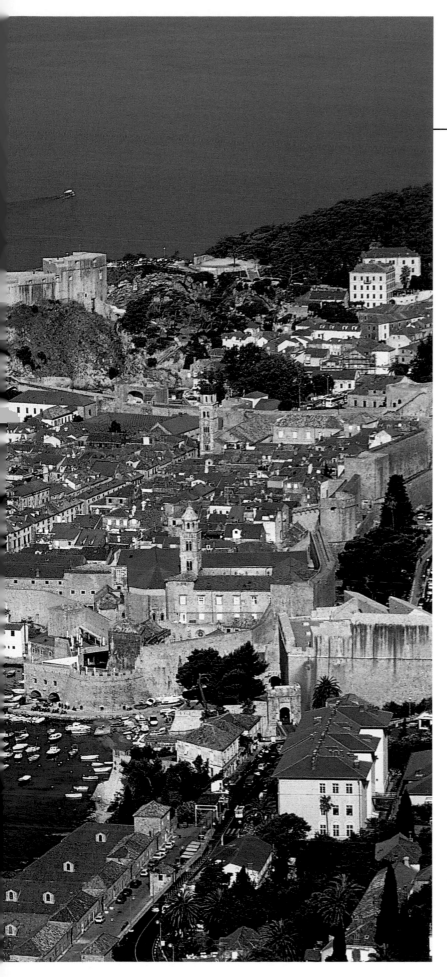

Dubrovnik

82-83 Dubrovnik is an unmissable destination for tourists to Croatia. It has been a UNESCO World Heritage site since 1979.

83 top left The Minceta tower, supported by walls and bastions, stands at the northeast corner of Dubrovnik's fortifications.

83 top right Pile Gate in Dubrovnik is the city's west gate.

83 bottom Dubrovnik's walls ring the old city. In some points they reach a thickness of 20 feet.

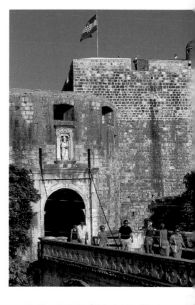

84-85 *A view over the roofs of Dubrovnik: the city was heavily bombed during the war for Croatian independence.*

85 top *The statue of St. Blaise (Sveti Vlaho) blesses the city from on high.*

85 center left *A detail of a Franciscan monastery. It contains one of Europe's oldest pharmacies, which has been open uninterruptedly since 1317.*

85 center right *The church of St. Blaise was rebuilt in 1715 after it had been destroyed by a fire. Its original Gothic features are no longer to be seen, having been replaced by a Baroque design, as seen in the façade.*

85 bottom *In the evening, the Loggia Square fills with people who come to take in its magical historical atmosphere.*

86-87 *The aerial view of Dubrovnik reveals the solidity of the city walls. They are just over a mile in length, 72 feet high and vary in thickness from 4'6" to 17'5".*

Parks

88 top Kopacki rit marsh is a national park 65 square miles large. Its reeds provide a habitat to 280 species of birds.

88 bottom Risnjak Park is 24 square miles large and mostly covered with woods.

89 This is one of the loveliest of the waterfalls in Plitvice Park. The Crna rijeka and Bijela rijeka rivers flow into the lakes.

Krka and Velebit

90 top left Krka river mostly flows through a canyon that reaches 660 feet in height. The river flows 45 miles on its course to the sea.

90 center left Two lakes form along the course of the Krka. Here we see a mill alongside the river.

90 bottom left Velebit Park has no human habitation at all.

90 top right Velebit Park lies at an altitude of 1,700 feet and stretches up to the peak of Mount Veliki Zavizan (5,500 feet).

90 center right Velebit was declared a protected area in 1999 to protect its unusual flora and landscape, the results of its particular morphology.

90 bottom right Visovac monastery stands on a small island in Visovac Lake.

91 The Krka river has seven waterfalls, including the Skradinski buk.

Plitvice

Risnjak National Park

94-95 *The name Risnjak is probably derived from ris which means lynx. Risnjak Park offers a habitat to many lynxes.*

95 top *The brown bear is a common animal in Gorski Kotar. It is often seen wandering near built-up areas and visits vegetable gardens in search of food.*

95 center left *The grass of the meadows contrasts with the green of the fir and beech trees.*

95 center right *The landscape in Risnjak Park is composed of rock masses, caverns, precipices and woods hundreds of years old.*

95 bottom *Summers in Gorski Kotar are sunny and cool and winters cold with plenty of snow.*

Kopacki rit
and Lonjsko polje

96 top The Eurasian bittern is just 16 inches long and one of the habitual inhabitants of Kopacki rit and Lonjsko polje parks.

96 center left The black tern nests where the Drava river flows into the Danube.

96 center right The unusual architecture in the photograph is typical of the houses in Posavina.

96 bottom A stork glides to its nest at the top of a roof. Usually storks build their nests on chimneys, and this is considered a good omen.

97 Kopacki rit Park is formed by pools, lakes and canals.

Istrian Peninsula

98 top Porec was built over a Roman castrum. The Roman decumanus has become the town's main street today.

98 bottom The Roman amphitheater in Pula dates to the first and second centuries. In terms of capacity (23,000 seats) and dimensions, it is one of the six largest Roman amphitheaters to survive to the present day.

99 The basilica of St. Euphemia overlooks Rovinj Hill. Like all the bell-towers in Istria, this one resembles the one in St. Mark's in Venice.

Porec

100-101 *Porec is one of Istria's largest tourist resorts. This is the historic center with the Euphrasian Basilica in the foreground.*

101 top left *The fourth-century Euphrasian Basilica was the first Christian building to be built in Istria.*

101 top right *The basilica's bell-tower stands beside the baptistery and was completed in 1522.*

101 center *The Euphrasian Basilica has a nave and two aisles; in the background we see the most important feature of the building – the apse.*

101 bottom *The Redeemer among the 12 apostles is the mosaic above the triumphal arch that leads into the apse of the Euphrasian Basilica.*

Rovinj

102-103 *The picturesque houses that face the sea here are in the port of Rovinj.*

103 top *Rovinj has a long marine tradition summed up in this photograph of a small fishing boat letting down its nets a short distance from the coast.*

103 center left *The tall, narrow houses in Rovinj nestle against one another in the manner typical of the Mediterranean. The chimneys on each house are different.*

103 center right *The legend goes that the sarcophagus of the fifth-century St. Euphemia was found on the beach of Rovinj.*

103 bottom *Rovinj is a maze of alleys and narrow streets that all lead towards the basilica of St. Euphemia up on the hill.*

Pula

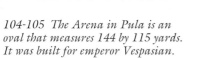

104-105 The Arena in Pula is an oval that measures 144 by 115 yards. It was built for emperor Vespasian.

104 bottom left After the Arena and Arch of the Sergi, a third of Pula's Roman monuments is the first century AD temple of Augustus, with its Corinthian colonnade.

104 bottom right At the time of Austro-Hungarian rule, Pula was an important military port due to its strategic location.

105 top Pula has conserved almost all of its many Roman remains intact which have been integrated into the fabric of the modern city.

105 center The inscription on Sergia's triumphal arch relates that it was built to honor the Sergia family on the wishes of the Roman lady Salvia Postuma.

105 bottom Santa Maria Formosa was a Byzantine basilica but today is a deconsecrated church. It was built in the eighth or ninth century next to a Benedictine Abbey but this is now in ruin.

Opatija Riviera

106 top left The park of Villa Angiolina (dated 1844) was the origin of Opatija. It lies near the Abbey (opatija in Croatian) of St. James after which the resort is named.

106 top right Volosko is composed of pretty little houses that were once fishermen's cottages.

106 center left The architecture of the palaces in Opatija includes Renaissance, Baroque and Neo-Classical styles. The town was a favorite summer and winter resort of the Austro-Hungarian nobility.

106 center right One of Opatija's loveliest hotels, the Millennium.

106 bottom Opatija's mild and healthy air means that exotic plants can grow. An important botanical event each year is the blooming of the camellias.

106-107 This is the dock in the pretty village of Volosko, which lies on the road between Opatija and Rijeka.

Rijeka

108 top The Palazzo Modello and city theater were designed by the architects Helmer and Fellner (who were also responsible for the theater in Zagreb). The palace is the seat of the Italian Union.

108 center Kobler Square lies in the middle of the historic center in the area known as the Old City of Rijeka.

108 bottom The cathedral of St. Vitus is reminiscent of the Venetian church of Santa Maria della Salute. It was designed in the seventeenth century by the Jesuit architect G. Briani.

108-109 Adria Square has identical fountains and is dominated by three important buildings: the Palazzo Adria, the Rijeka Skyscraper and the modern Bank Building.

Inland Istria

110-111 *Perched on a hill, Motovun is a lovely village overlooking the surrounding countryside. Its streets have not lost their medieval appearance.*

111 *Groznjan was once an administrative center in Venetian Istria. Today it has become a center for young musicians from around the world.*

112 A field of poppies: a note of color in the Istrian countryside northwest of Opatija. In the background there are the vines that produce Istria's excellent wines.

113 The countryside of Istria with its plots of land. In autumn truffles grow along the valley of the Mirna river.

The Pearls of the Adriatic

114 top The island of Brac is famous for its many tiny beaches and the quarries that provided the stone used to build Diocletian's Palace in Split.

114 bottom This is the marina in Cres on the bare and stony island of the same name. Heading south the Mediterranean scrub is seen once more. Two features of the island are the dry walls and free-ranging flocks of sheep.

115 On the tiny St. Mary's island at Mljet, which lies in one of the two lakes (Veliko jezero) joined to the sea, the Benedictine monastery has been transformed into a hotel. The surrounding area is a nature park.

Pag and Rab

116 top The attractive twelfth–thirteenth-century Romanesque bell-tower was built separate from the church of the Madonna. The church contains a treasure and ancient inventory.

116 center left The capital town, Pag, stands on the gulf of the same name, which is closed on one side by a beach and on the other by famous salt-mines. The town is also known for its muds.

116 center right A lace-worker makes a pillow. The lace products of Pag are renowned and costly.

116 bottom An aerial view of the island of Pag shows the harshness of the land, which is suitable only for raising sheep.

116-117 Rab is a peaceful town that has a pleasant Mediterranean climate and plenty of beaches. The villages of Lopar, Supetar and Kampor also lie on the island.

Brac, Vis, Kornati and Dugi otok

118-119 An aerial photograph of Kornati archipelago. The entire archipelago covers 86 square miles.

119 top left Bol is the best seaside resort in Dalmatia. This is the famous Zlatni Rat (Golden Point) beach that thrusts into the sea like a wedge and changes shape with the currents.

119 top right The island of Vis is one of those most distant from the coast. Its largest town (in the picture) is Komiza. Historically the island is remembered for the naval battle between the Italians and Austrians in 1866.

119 center The karstic terrain of the islands allows the cultivation of grapes and olives. Here we see the pine trees on the island of Brac.

119 bottom Dugi Otok (Long Island) is also called Sali for the salt-mines it used to have. Fishing provides the inhabitants main income due to the depth of the water and richness of the sea.

Mljet and Korcula

120 *The town of Korcula (in the photograph) still has its walls and towers. The treasure-filled cathedral is dedicated to St. Mark.*

121 top *The coast of Korcula is lined by a series of inlets and, on the south coast, cliffs up to 100 feet high.*

121 bottom *The 'Moreska' is a traditional dance in costume that originated in the fifteenth century.*

122 *Much of the island of Mljet is covered by pine woods, and there are only about ten villages.*

123 *A Benedictine abbey dominates the island of Mljet. Here we see the tower and the Romanesque church.*

Hvar

124 The island of Hvar produces great wines. Here a farmer cares for one of the vines on his land.

125 The climate of Hvar is very mild and suitable for holidays all year round. There are many towns and villages, some of which are hidden in the Mediterranean scrub.

126-127 The island abounds in aromatic herbs. Here we see the harvesting of the lavender from which the plants' oil is extracted.